ISBN 978-1-332-73404-7
PIBN 10297896

1 MONTH OF
FREE
READING

at

www.ForgottenBooks.com

By purchasing this book you are
eligible for one month membership to
ForgottenBooks.com, giving you
unlimited access to our entire
collection of over 700,000 titles via
our web site and mobile apps.

To claim your free month visit:

www.forgottenbooks.com/free297896

English
Français
Deutsche
Italiano
Español
Português

www.forgottenbooks.com

Mythology Photography **Fiction**
Fishing Christianity **Art** Cooking
Essays Buddhism Freemasonry
Medicine **Biology** Music **Ancient
Egypt** Evolution Carpentry Physics
Dance Geology **Mathematics** Fitness
Shakespeare **Folklore** Yoga Marketing
Confidence Immortality Biographies
Poetry **Psychology** Witchcraft
Electronics Chemistry History **Law**
Accounting **Philosophy** Anthropology
Alchemy Drama Quantum Mechanics
Atheism Sexual Health **Ancient History**
Entrepreneurship Languages Sport
Paleontology Needlework Islam
Metaphysics Investment Archaeology
Parenting Statistics Criminology
Motivational

Things
As They Are

Ballads

by
Berton Braley
Author of "Songs of the Workaday World"

New York
George H. Doran Company

TO
MY MOTHER

MY thanks and acknowledgments are due to the following magazines and publishers for permission to use these poems in book form:

Munsey's Magazine, Ainslee's, Woman's World, The Anode, The Ladies' World, Motor Print, Popular Magazine, Short Story Publishing Co., Illustrated Sunday Magazines, Collier's Weekly, Newspaper Enterprise Association, The Saturday Evening Post, All Around, New York World, New York Tribune, United Press, The Caxton, Pacific Monthly, The Cavalier, Youth's Companion, Woman's Magazine, McClure's Magazine, Puck, Judge, The Century, Life, Metropolitan.

CONTENTS

CONTENTS

THE LITTLE THINGS WE CARE

DOWN IN THE CROWD

THOSE BENEATH THE HARROW

SAVOUR OF SALT

CONTENTS

BALLADS OF WHAT YOU PLEASE

THE BREATH IN THE CLAY

THE SINGER'S DEFIANCE

Life, you have harried and hurt and scourged me,
  Mocked me cruelly through the years.
Under a burden of woe submerged me,
  Sought to fright me with pain and tears,
Fortune and glory you have denied me,
  Love you gave me—and took away,
Yet, for all of the years you've tried me,
  Dauntless I sing to the world today.

For out of the wreck of a vanished passion,
  Out of the failure, the doubt, the pain,
Out of the sorrow and death I'll fashion
  Many a song in a fearless strain,
And the songs I make shall have no savor
  Of useless longing or vain regret,
But I shall carol to make men braver
  For every trial that must be met.

Failure, defeat, despair—I know them,
  But still I challenge them, unafraid,
And men shall battle and overthrow them,
  Perchance because of a song I've made;
Life—though my peace and my joy be taken,
  Though all my visions and dreams go by,
I'll lift my voice in a tone unshaken
  And keep on singing until I die!

THE POINT OF VIEW

HE had toiled in the furnace glare
  Where the white hot metal glows,
He had done a grader's share
  In the road camp's dust and snows,
He had known the deep mines' murk
  And the threat of the lurking damp.
He had sweated at sailors' work
  On the decks of a deep-sea tramp.

So, having some gift of song,
  He sang of these chaps he knew,
A chant of the toiling throng
  With the world's rough jobs to do,
And the critics said, "Ah yes,
  Here's a note that is loud enough
To curry some cheap success
  With people who like such stuff.

"As jingles they're fairly wrought,
  But they do not smack of the soil,
For this troubadour hasn't caught
  The spirit and soul of toil."
And the singer read—and grinned
  And the workers, fagged and spent,
Sweating and grimy skinned,
  Knew not what the critics meant.

THE POINT OF VIEW (continued)

But the singer's songs they knew,
And it was to *them* he sang;
And if *they* found them true—
To hell with the critic gang!

SUCCESS

IF you want a thing bad enough
　　To go out and fight for it,
Work day and night for it,
Give up your time and your peace and your sleep for it,
If only desire of it
Makes you quite mad enough
Never to tire of it,
Makes you hold other things tawdry and cheap for it;
If life seems all empty and useless without it
And all that you scheme and you dream is about it,
If gladly you'll sweat for it,
Fret for it,
Plan for it,
Lose all your terror of God or of man for it,
If you'll simply go after that thing that you want,
With all your capacity,
Strength and sagacity,
Faith, hope and confidence, stern pertinacity,
If neither cold poverty, famished and gaunt,
Nor sickness nor pain
Of body or brain
Can turn you away from the thing that you want,
If dogged and grim you besiege and beset it,
You'll get it!

THE FAILURES

WE were busy making money
　　In the world's great game;
We were "gathering the honey"
　　When the vision came.
We greeted it with laughter,
　　Though we frowned upon
"The fools" who followed after,
　　When the dream had gone!

Oh, we were canny schemers,
　　So we sold and bought;
And jeered the silly dreamers
　　And the dream they sought.
We gave but fleeting glances
　　To that "hare-brained crew,"
For we took no stock in fancies—
　　Till the dream came true!

So much had gold imbued us,
　　So had greed been nursed,
We'd let the Best elude us
　　And we'd kept the Worst;
We long to "do it over,"
　　But we cannot try,
For every dream's a rover,
　　And our dream's gone by!

SPURS

MY foes, they are my dearest friends;
　　They save me from placidity;
They free my life, its aims and ends,
　　Of sloth and pale vapidity;
They wake me from my dullest doze
　　And force me to my job again;
They keep me always on my toes,
　　Alive, alert, athrob again!

My foes!　They jeer my smug conceit,
　　Which I am fondly nourishing;
They chasten me with loss, defeat,
　　When luck becomes too flourishing.
I dare not halt in my advance
　　Or shirk things with impunity;
My foes would see in such a chance
　　A golden opportunity.

My friends—the debt to them is great;
　　Their love and faith I'm treasuring,
But it's my foes who hold me straight
　　And help me past all measuring;
They keep me always "in the pink."
　　A stimulant their venom is,
Which makes me strong and "fit."　I drink
　　A health unto mine enemies!

THE OUTCAST

THEY called him "fool" and "traitor"
  As through the land he went;
They cried out "agitator"
  And "brand of discontent!"
From altar and from steeple
  Upon this man forlorn
The priests and "better people"
  Hurled wrath and cruel scorn.

They called him "cheat" and "faker,"
  And drove him from the door;
They shouted, "Mischiefmaker,
  Begone and come no more!"
From border unto border
  They hounded him, lest he
"Upset established order
  And bring on Anarchy!"

At length they seized and tried him,
  That they might have their will,
And so they crucified him
  Upon a lonely hill,
The outcast agitator
  Driven by scourge and rod;
They called him "fool" and "traitor."
  We call him Son of God!

GIFTS

MAY these be yours.....
The Gifts that make the Dreamers into
Doers,
The Gift to work
Through Joy and Sorrow, Light or Murk,
To play, with all your soul and heart,
A manly part!

The Gift of Discontent, to keep you driving
Forward and up, forever striving
For something better in the days hereafter;
The Gift of Kindness and the Gift of Laughter,
And all the gifts of Love and Faith and Friends,
Of Justice and of Truth,
And in your heart, until life's journey ends,
The Priceless Gift of Youth,
Hope that inspires and Courage that endures,
May all these Gifts be Yours!

THE CONQUEROR

ROOM for me, graybeards, room, make room!
Menace me not with your eyes of gloom;
Jostle me not from the place I seek,
For my arms are strong and your own are weak,
And if my plea to you be denied
I'll thrust your wearying forms aside.
Pity you? Yes, but I cannot stay;
I am the spirit of Youth; make way!

Room for me, timid ones, room, make room!
Little I care for your fret and fume—
I dare whatever is mine to meet,
I laugh at sorrow and jeer defeat;
To doubt and doubters I give the lie,
And fear is stilled as I swagger by,
And life's a fight and I seek the fray;
I am the spirit of Youth; make way!

Room for me, mighty ones, room, make room!
I fear no power and dread no doom;
And you who curse me or you who bless
Alike must bow to my dauntlessness.
I topple the king from his golden throne,
I smash old idols of brass and stone,
I am not hampered by yesterday.
Room for the spirit of Youth; make way!

THE CONQUEROR (continued)

Room for me, all of you, make me room!
Where the rifles crash and the cannon boom,
Where glory beckons or love or fame
I plunge me heedlessly in the game.
The old, the wary, the wise, the great,
They cannot stay me, for I am Fate,
The brave young master of all good play,
I am the spirit of Youth; make way!

A PRAYER

LORD, let me live like a Regular Man,
　　With Regular friends and true;
Let me play the game on a Regular plan
　　And play it that way all through;
Let me win or lose with a Regular smile
　　And never be known to whine,
For that is a "Regular Fellow's" style
　　And I want to make it mine!

Oh, give me a Regular chance in life,
　　The same as the rest, I pray,
And give me a Regular Girl for wife
　　To help me along the way;
Let us know the lot of humanity,
　　Its regular woes and joys,
And raise a Regular family
　　Of Regular girls and boys!

Let me live to a Regular good old age,
　　With Regular snow-white hair,
Having done my labor and earned my wage
　　And played my game for fair;
And so at last when the people scan
　　My face on its peaceful bier,
They'll say, "Well, he was a Regular Man!"
　　And drop a Regular tear!

MURK O   PIT

AT A WAR HOSPITAL

DOCTOR, here's a man without a jaw;
    Doctor, here's a chap without a cheek,
Battered up by shrapnel, bleeding raw,
    Smelling of the battle's smoke and reek;
Doctor, here's a leg that's torn to scraps;
    Here's a hand that's hanging by a thread.
What's the final verdict on these chaps
    Waiting while their bandages grow red?

Well, they're not pleasant to look at—covered with
    vermin and mud,
Battered and mangled and shattered, scarlet or black-
    ened with blood;
Still it's our business to mend them, build them all over
    again,
Forming these terrible fragments back into brothers
    and men;
Framing a jawbone of rubber, growing a cheek from a
    scar;
Routing the germs of infection, fighting the horrors of
    war,
All of our training and science meeting the instant de-
    mand,
Wasting no moments in pity—pity unsteadies the
    hand—
Calm and unfeeling and certain, knowing the things
    we must do.
Such is the work of the surgeon—making men over
    anew!

AT A WAR HOSPITAL (continued)

    Here's a chap that's torn from head to heels;
      Death has got him hanging on the brink,
    Yet he always answers that he feels
      Simply "In the pink, sir, in the pink!"
    Grinning if they have a mouth to grin,
      Winking very gaily if it's gone;
    That's the kind of men they're bringing in;
      That's the type of lad we're working on.

Yet we must take them as "cases"—work that is here
    to be done,
Each as a sort of a battle—struggle that has to be won,
Smashed by the scattering shrapnel, hand grenades,
    bullets and shells,
Victims of gunfire and gases worse than a number of
    hells;
These are the fellows we tackle, taking what fragments
    there be,
Forming them back into humans fit for their sweet-
    hearts to see,
Splicing their nerves and their muscles, rebuilding tis-
    sue and bone,
Making strange surgical magic hitherto almost un-
    known;
There is a joy in our labors, though they are grisly
    to do;
We are the miracle workers—making men over anew!

THE CIGARETTE

CHARGED by reformers with horrible qualities,
Railed at as "Coffin Nail, Dope Stick," and such,
Painted as tainted with vast criminalities,
Filling up jails with the folk in its clutch;
Yet it leaves some of us owning our sanity,
Some of us free from the prisons awhile,
For, though it's viewed as a foe to humanity,
Maybe the cigarette isn't so vile!

Maybe it's sometimes a solace for care
Floating our troubles off into the air;
Maybe it isn't as deadly as "Coke."
Maybe it isn't a crime—but a smoke.

Prospectors roaming the hills solitarily,
Cowboys who ride over limitless plains,
Hunters who creep through the jungle murk warily,
Trailbreakers toiling with muscles and brains—
Men such as these find a calm and benignity
Out of the fumes of the "vile cigarette."
Not in their minds does it stand for malignity,
Rather for comfort and surcease from fret.

Blithely they puff on each rice paper roll,
Cheerful of countenance, placid of soul.
Cigarette terrors to them are a joke;
They've never thought it a crime—but a smoke!

THE CIGARETTE (continued)

Down in the trenches where shrapnel is spattering,
   Down where the rifle fire crackles and rips,
'Mid all the stenches, the tumult ear-shattering,
   Men still can grin with a "nail" in their lips,
Making the pain of the wounded more bearable,
   Calming the surgeon for tasks to be met.
This, in the war, is the work of the terrible
   "Bait of the devil, the vile cigarette!"

Blessing of conflict—and when that shall cease,
Maybe a balm in the bringing of peace;
Maybe it's not such a menace to folk;
Maybe it isn't a crime—but a smoke!

THE FIGHTERS

FOOLS cried: "Alas, that valor is no more,
   That men grow timid, soft, effeminate,
That strength and fortitude degenerate,
And all the sterner virtues passed of yore!"
Their wail was swallowed in the cannon's roar,
   The nations grappled in a grip of hate,
   And men by millions marched to meet their fate,
Valiant and fearless in the wrath of war.

Machine guns belched with murder on their breath;
   The shrapnel burst and heaped the dead in hills;
Time had not known such carnival of death.
   Yet still, with dauntless hearts and dogged wills,
Men battled on. In earth's grim histories,
There never were such fighting men as these!

THE LITTLE PRIEST OF SOISSONS

THE little priest of Soissons
    Toils in the war's red wake.
His eyes are filled with sorrow;
    His heart is one dull ache,
But still he smiles most tenderly
    For his Dear Master's sake.

His frock is splashed and muddy,
    And weary are his feet,
But ever gentle are his hands,
    His voice forever sweet;
And dying soldiers smile to hear
    The prayers his lips repeat.

The little priest of Soissons
    Has met his people's need.
His is a soul beyond all caste,
    All blood, or race, or breed;
He labors only to fulfill
    The Saviour's simple creed.

The lands are torn with conflict,
    The skies are bleak above,
But mid the desolation stands
    The quiet figure of
The little priest of Soissons,
    Whose only thought is love!

TARNISHED

A GERMAN soldier, wearing on his breast
The Iron Cross, of all things he possessed

The dearest, since it had been bravely won
By splendid deeds of valor, nobly done,

Sat in a trench amid the field guns' din
And read a month-old paper from Berlin.

The Kaiser, so he learned, had given to
A submarine commander and his crew

The Iron Cross, because with courage great
They sent an unarmed liner to her fate

And thus upheld the Fatherland's renown
By leaving women and their babes to drown.

By this brave news his soldier heart was stirred,
And then he read, "The cross has been conferred

On many gallant airmen, who displayed
Such valor in the last Zeppelin raid

When bombs were dropped and English blood was
spilled
And fifteen mothers with their babes were killed."

TARNISHED (continued)

A choking sound escaped the soldier's throat;
He tore the Iron Cross from off his coat,

Flung it to earth, and with a muttered "Gott!"
Stamped it in mud and spat upon the spot!

CHANT ROYAL OF WAR

WITH lances raised the troopers thunder by
    And in the sun their polished helmets flare;
A mass of surging color fills the eye,
    The pennons dip, the brazen trumpets blare;
The infantry, in marching row on row,
Comes swinging past, a brave and sightly show,
    And in the wake of all this massed array
    The grim, forbidding field guns lurch and sway;
The echo of the cheers resounds afar,
    And fools look on this pageantry and say,
"Behold the glory and the pomp of War!"

Thus Emperors and Kings and rulers high
    Send forth their nations' Youth to do and dare;
And how shall humble soldiers question Why?
    The War Lords call, and War is their affair.
Let lovers kiss and cling before they go,
For what the future holds no man may know.
    The children wail, the wives and mothers pray,
    Fearful of all the menace of the fray,
Of lives and loves that war will wreck or mar;
    Only as tawdry shams and lies do they
Behold the glory and the pomp of War!

About deserted fields the blackbirds fly,
    The grain is rotting and the barns are bare,
The shops are empty and the winepress dry,
    The mills are silent, and the furnace glare

CHANT ROYAL OF WAR (continued)

Has died to ashes. Creakingly and slow
The ships sway at their hawsers to and fro,
    Denied the salty deeps and flying spray;
    The clutch of famine tightens day by day,
Disease comes stalking where the helpless are
    (Starving and gaunt, with faces pinched and gray)—
Behold the glory and the pomp of War!

Houses and palaces and churches lie
    In ruins beyond mending or repair;
War tramples on, though Art and Beauty die
    Under his feet that crush, his hands that tear;
The horror and the desolation grow;
War's track is black as if a molten flow
    Of seething lava followed on his way.
    The beast in Man breaks every bond and stay
And gorges foully without let or bar.
    What minstrel hymns these exploits in his lay?
Behold the glory and the pomp of War!

The thunder of the cannon fills the sky
    And shrapnel hurtles shrieking through the air;
Men answer battle cry with battle cry
    And fall in windrows with their eyes astare.
Red, red the sun seems, with a hateful glow
That beats upon the shambles down below
    And lifts a stench of corpses and decay;
    Here is no bright parade, no pageant gay,
But bloodlust ruled by some malevolent star
    Which drives men on to slay and slay and slay.
Behold the glory and the pomp of War!

CHANT ROYAL OF WAR (continued)

L'Envoi

Some time, somewhere, my Masters, ye shall **pay**
  For all the Wrath and Evil ye let play
While ye stayed safely, free of wound or scar,
  And in the Blackness of the Pit ye may
Behold the glory and the pomp of War!

THE GLAMOUR

NOW when I worked in the factory I tended a
rattling loom,
And hour by hour and day by day in the same old fac-
tory room
I did my job in the same old way till my body and soul
were sick,
Sick of the task that never changed in a shop where the
air was thick.

Then when night time came, why, I plodded home to
the same old cheerless place,
With the same old smells and the same old food and
the same old want of space.
I was undernourished and overworked and I had no
cash to spend
And life went on in a routine round that had no pause
or end.

There was nothing to give my heart a thrill or waken
my brain to fire,
There was nothing to stir my weary soul to passion
or joy or ire,
Till sudden the trumpets blew for war and something
within me stirred,
And I took my place with the fighting men who
marched at the fighting word.

THE GLAMOUR (continued)

I have charged at death and been afraid, and con-
quered my fear and fought;
I have been in the midst of a hundred hells where the
guns their havoc wrought;
I have stood knee deep in the trench's mud with a frost-
white fog for breath;
I have smoked and jested and fought with men; I have
seen them go to death.

I know not when I shall meet my fate in the fields that
the cannon plow,
But I'm tasting adventure high and great, and I know
I am *living* now,
Not shuffling about at a weary stint on a linty factory
floor,—
Yet people wonder why men like me should answer
the call to war!

THE WARRIOR

THE women toil in the fields all day,
The children tend to the flocks that stray,
The dust is thick on the merchant's till,
And forge and furnace are cold and still;
The maidens sigh and the young wives weep,
While mothers suffer in anguish deep,
But on to battle with head held high
Youth goes valiantly forth to die!

Youth o'erflowing
With careless song,
Youth the glowing,
The blithe, the strong,
Gaily flouting
Its foes afar,
Youth goes shouting
Away to war!

The trees are shattered, the fields are black,
And famine stalks in the armies' track;
The wounded groan in their bitter pain
And the trenches fill with a host of slain;
But Youth fights on in the face of Hell,
Of singing bullet and shrieking shell,
With eyes that smoulder and lips gone dry
Youth goes doggedly forth to die!

THE WARRIOR (continued)

> Age may censure
> And Love may thrall
> But Youth will venture
> In spite of all,
> For peace seems hollow
> And dull and stale
> And Youth must follow
> The trumpet's hail!

When the bugles blow and the war drums beat
Youth thrills to the tramp of the soldiers' feet,
And only in conflict finds the meed
Of high adventure and reckless deed.
The Cause?—no matter! The End?—who cares?
It's War's Great Game to the man who dares!
The women wail and the wise men sigh
But Youth goes gallantly forth to die!

THE WANDERER'S WAY

THE OLD CALL

HARRIGAN came home again; he said he'd never
     roam again,
  He'd had enough of wandering, adventure and ro-
     mance;
His life had been an olio of battle and imbroglio,
  A calendar of danger and a chronicle of chance;
But now, in all sobriety, he swore he'd found satiety,
  He'd had his fill of struggle in the lands of east and
     west.
"Me one desire," said Harrigan, "is just an easy chair
     again,
  A pipe, a pair of slippers and a lot of time to rest."

Harrigan came home again to tread the common loam
     again—
  "I long to loaf about," he said, "and let me girth
     increase,
To settle down complacently and quietly and dacently
  Where everything is orderly and all the ways are
     peace!"
Yet though he ceased from traveling his tongue would
     keep unraveling
  A golden string of stories of the roving days gone
     by,
And in the eyes of Harrigan a sudden flame would
     flare again,
  And from the breast of Harrigan would issue forth
     a sigh!

THE OLD CALL (continued)

Harrigan came home again—but far across the foam
    again
  The old red god of slaughter called his millions to
    the fray.
And Harrigan? Why, Harrigan, he sniffed the ambient
    air again,
  Forgot his vows of peacefulness and started on his
    way.
Time never can diminish it and only death can finish it,
  The magic of adventure which is strong beyond our
    ken;
And so it is with Harrigan, who's off to do and dare
    again,
  To taste the smoke of battle and to play the game
    with Men!

THE BEACH COMBERS

WE'VE wandered far from home, sweet home,
    That dear remembered spot,
Where some of us were gentlemen
    And most of us were not;
We've trod the path of dalliance
    And trudged the rover's trail;
We've spent some time in Arcady
    But more of it in jail!

Oh, women wait for some of us,
    And wardens wait for more,
But still we drift about the world
    From lazy shore to shore:
For we have felt the tropic's spell,
    And, spite of every call,
We cannot drive our drowsy souls
    To free us from the thrall!

The waving of the fronded palms,
    The sleepy hush at noon,
The wonder of the tropic night,
    The magic of the moon,
The breakers on the coral beach
    That tumble into foam—
By these enchantments we are bound:
    You cannot call us home!

THE LAWLESS HEART

DULL trade hath bound me in its grip
　　And never shall I be free,
Yet I dream of the decks of a pirate ship
　　In the roll of the open sea;
I dream of the pennant dread and black
　　That flies at the mast alway,
As we swoop along on a Merchant's track
　　In the sting of the flying spray!

Oh, I am a law abiding chap,
　　Yet deep in my heart I'd be
A buccaneer with a scarlet cap
　　And a Terror of the Sea,
As lawless and ruthless a bandit brute
　　As history ever knew,
Roaming the seas in search of loot
　　At the head of an evil crew!

Oh, here at home I am meek and mild,
　　A man with a family,
Yet I dream of deeds that were dark and wild,
　　And of red, red fights at sea;
And under my breath I softly hum
　　A stave from a pirate song,
And my throat grows parched for pirate rum—
　　For I have been dry so long!

THE LAWLESS HEART (continued)

My life is ordered and shaped and bound
    And kept to its rule and line,
But my thoughts can wander the whole world round
    And my dreams—my dreams are mine!
So the old tales hold me in their grip
    And I hungrily long to be
A pirate chief on a low black ship
    In the roll of the open sea!

NAMES OF ROMANCE

AROUND the good world's wide expanse
  Are places great and small,
Whose names fair tingle with romance—
  And I would see them all:
There's Cairo, Fez and Ispahan,
  Bangkok and Singapore,
And Trebizonde and Cagayan
  And Rio and Lahore.

There's Sarawak and Callao
  Algiers and Kandahar,
Khartoum, Rangoon and Tokio,
  Bombay and Zanzibar;
About the name of each there clings
  Enchantment's golden veil,
The wonder of strange folk and things,
  The glamour of the trail!

For some are north and some are south
  And some are east and west,
And some are cursed with heat and drouth
  And some with balm are blessed;
But Capetown, Rhodes or Disco Bay,
  Shanghai, Seville or Rome,
Their names come singing down the way
  To tempt me forth from home,
Their magic's ringing down the way,
  To lure me forth from home!

SOMEBODY

SOMEBODY'S got to be steady
  And stick at a regular job,
Somebody's got to be ready
  To stay with the laboring mob.

Somebody's got to be trudging
  The path from the house to the mill,
Somebody's got to be drudging
  At work that has never a thrill.

Every one cannot be left to roam
  Careless and blithe and free,
Somebody's got to stay at home,
  Somebody *Else*—not me!

THE SAILOR'S RETURN

I LEFT the sea "forever,"
  I broke her ancient thrall,
I would have done with rolling deeps
  And decks that rise and fall;
But up the roads I travel
  And on the very breeze
There follows, follows, follows
  The spell that is the sea's.

The clouds that hang above me
  Are islands in a blue
As clear as tropic waters
  That I have idled through,
And every flowing river
  Is like the changing tide
That fills the salt sea marshes
  Along the ocean side.

The wind among the wheat-fields
  Makes billows in the grain,
Like stately deep-sea gray-backs
  That lift and sink again;
By day I can't escape her,
  And in the night it seems
I walk a reeling freighter
  And sail the sea in dreams.

THE SAILOR'S RETURN (continued)

She smiles at me in picture,
　　She calls to me in song,
For painter folk and poet folk
　　Have served her well and long;
And is her magic broken,
　　Her glamour from me hurled?
Nay, once again upon a ship
　　I'll sail across the world!

RUINED

ONCE he was a wanderer, once he was a fighter,
  Once he was a knight of high romance,
Following Adventure just as far as he could sight her,
  Plunging life and fortune on a chance!

Once he diced with destiny, truculent and merry,
  Once he roved the world by land and sea;
Now he rides contentedly on the Jersey ferry,
  Commonplace and placid as can be.

Once he was a rover and a prince of princely men,
  Leading fights or frolickings with vim;
Now he nods at dinner and he goes to bed at ten,
  And that's what Mr. Cupid's done to him!

THE FREE COURSE

NOT mine the track of a star in space
    Which must keep to its course on high,
With never a chance for a swifter pace
    Or a romp in the vasty sky;

Though the star be safe and the star hold true
    I would rather be wholly free
To run amuck in the heavenly blue,
    So—the comet's course for me,

To leap in leaps of a billion miles
    'Mid the stars of the milky way,
And to play hop skotch through the stellar aisles
    In a boisterous mood of play!

If I were a star I would quickly tire
    Of a path that was fixed and tame,
And I'd whoop through space with a tail of fire
    And burst in a flare of flame!

THE LITTLE THINGS WE
ABOUT

THE DEAD DREAM

WHEN the dream is dead and its magic flown
  Bare is the branch where the rose has grown,
And the songs and laughter are hushed and still
And the blood runs slow and the heart grows chill,
Like an empty house and a hearth wind-blown.

When the dream is dead, Love makes his moan
For the vanished joy that he once has known,
  And his voice is choked and his deep eyes fill.

Romance is shattered and overthrown.
And grim despair, with a face of stone,
  Makes work turn weary and life run ill,
  Robbed of the glow, the flame, the thrill—
For the body lives, but the Soul has flown,
    When the dream is dead!

THE HOUSE OF DREAMS

I WANT a house by the sea
  In the drench of the whirling spume,
Where the wild white breakers boom
  And the wind blows salt and free,

Bearing a song to me
  Of the wide, wide ocean spaces,
Of headland and isle and key
  And a myriad magic places;
I want a house by the sea.

I want a house by the sea,
  Where the white gulls dip and fly,
  And the "lordly ships go by"
On cruises of mystery;

A house built strong for the rages
  Of tempest and shrieking storm;
A house to stand for the ages,
  Sturdy and staunch and warm,
To shelter my dog and my books and me—
And my Love, when love shall come to me.
  I want a house by the sea!

CURTAIN

AND so we part in friendship, yes,
   With neither pain nor bitterness,
And, unbewitched, we plainly see
The meaning of our comedy;
Yet this we know—and, knowing, smile,
'At least we loved a little while!

The vows we made, the faith we swore
To love—and love forevermore,
Are quite forgot; we turn and go
Certain, that it is better so.
Yet though Romance cannot beguile,
At least we loved a little while.

Because you loved me, I have known
A world I could not find alone,
And from my love did you not gain
A glimpse of palaces in Spain?
What if we missed the Blissful Isle,
At least we loved a little while.

Good-by—upon your brow I press
The kiss of faithful friendliness,
For though we part from sorrow free,
We lived a space in Arcady,
'And we can whisper, with a smile,
"At least we loved a Little While!"

[61]

GREETING

WHEN Jill comes down the lane,
  Her eyes alight with laughter,
Her lips like cherries twain,
  Her blown hair floating after,
So airy seem her ways,
  So fine her flying tresses,
I think of elves and fays
  And Dresden shepherdesses.

When Jill comes down the lane,
  So dryad-like and slender,
There follows in her train
  A sort of faery splendor;
She brings, she brings to me,
  With all her wistful graces,
A breath of Arcady,
  A lilt of sunlit spaces.

When Jill comes down the lane
  (How blue the skies above her!)
I give my thanks again,
  Because—because I love her.
How shall I make it plain—
  My joy to have her greet me?
Ah, words are more than vain,
When Jill comes down the lane,
  Comes down the lane to meet me!

THE WARNING

KEEP away from women, boy,
  And play a lonely game,
For the bad ones make you crooked
  And the good ones make you tame;
They want to keep you sheltered
  From the stress and storm of chance,
And they hold you from Adventure
  By the spell of soft Romance.

Keep away from women, boy;
  They either break your heart
With falseness and with mockery
  And coldly cruel art,
Or else with clinging kisses
  And fond and loving charm,
They keep you from the struggle
  And spoil your fighting arm!

Keep away from women, boy,
  Wherever they may lurk;
They make your courage falter,
  And they play the deuce with work;
They weave you silken fetters
  Which are stronger far than steel;
They rob your soul of daring
  And your heart and brain of zeal!

THE WARNING (continued)

Keep away from women, boy,
 And shun their loveliness,
And you shall tread unswervingly
 The pathway to success;
The world shall call you Master
 And fortune heed your call,
And you shall reach the lonely heights—
 And never *Live* at all!

IMPATIENCE

WAIT!" do you say?   But my arms fairly ache
     for you—
Och, but the waiting is dreary and long!
Sweet, the old heart of me's ready to break for you;
    Sure, and the wish for you's growing more strong!
Faith, I get mad for the sound and the sight of you,
    Ay, and the touch of your head on my breast,
AND the feel of your hand and the kisses so light of
    you—
    "Wait!" do you say?—and "It's all for the best."

"Wait!" do you say?   But I'm burning with fire for
    you,
    Crying aloud for you nighttime and day;
AND my body and soul are athrill with desire for
    you,
    Wasting me swiftly and surely away.
"Wait!" do you say?   Is the heart of you numb to me?
    Where is your pity, love,—vanished and flown?
Och, but I love you; oh, come to me, come to me!
    "Wait!" do you say?   But I'm wanting My Own!

THE LASTING LOOK

WHEN a pretty girl goes by
 There's a glimmer in my eye,
Just a flicker of delight
At so glad and fair a sight;
Youth and beauty and romance
These are what my roving glance
Find in every curve and curl
Of a passing pretty girl,
And my heart is beating high
When a lovely maid goes by.

If I yield me to her charm
As she passes, where's the harm?
I'll not follow her, or speak
Words to flush that peach-blow cheek,
But my much-adoring gaze
Dwells upon her as she sways
Daintily a-down the street
Gay and very blithe and sweet.
Love of beauty's not amiss;
Who shall censure me for this?

If I ever get so I
Care not as the girls go by,
If no glance of mine shall rest
On the very prettiest—

THE LASTING LOOK (continued)

> Take me quickly then, I pray,
> And just bury me away,
> For, though I may breathe and move,
> My indifference will prove
> That the life has gone from me
> And I'm dead as dead can be.

DOWN IN THE CROWD

THE METROPOLIS

NEW YORK—it is a chary town,
   A canny and a wary town,
But still a blithe and merry town to those who love it
     well,
   A noisy town, a blary town,
   A cruel, a contrary town,
And yet an airy, fairy town which casts a magic spell.

   New York—it is a funny town,
   A sad, a dark, a sunny town,
A simply-mad-for-money town—or so the cynics cry;
   A place of greed and charity,
   Of famine and prosperity,
Where life moves with celerity and time goes sweep-
     ing by.

   New York—it is a gritty town,
   A dull town and a witty town,
An ugly and a pretty town, a dreary town or gay;
   It's quiet and it's clamorous,
   It's practical and glamorous,
It's loveless and it's amorous—it's anything you say!

   New York—a most capricious town,
   A godly and a vicious town,

THE METROPOLIS (continued)

A true and meretricious town, a town of peace and
    strife,
  Of sober worth and vanity,
  Of rudeness and urbanity,
As varied as humanity—illogical as life!

THE STREET PIANO

THE clamor and hurry of people who scurry
　On myriad missions of good or of ill,
The deep diapason of traffic that plays on
　The streets of a city which never is still—
These sounds cannot swing me from labors that bring
　　me
　The fat little envelope Saturday noon;
And yet I start humming when gaily is strumming
　The loud street piano that jangles a tune.

Let those who will do so applaud at Caruso,
　Go wild over Hofmann and others of note,
But me for the straying pianoman's playing
　That steals to my ear on the breezes afloat,
With sad tunes and bad tunes and mad tunes and glad
　　tunes,
　With popular ditties that often repeat,
And I, with my pencil or some such utensil,
　Keep tapping my desk to the tune in the street.

My figures grow hazy, I gaze with a lazy
　And indolent languor at nothing at all,
In happy enslavement while up from the pavement
　The magical melodies summon and call.
They build me a vision of meadows Elysian,
　Of brooklets that babble and breezes that croon,
And, wistful and tender, young Spring in her splendor
　Comes dancing to me on the wings of a tune!

SHADE AND LIGHT

WHEN it's cloudy in the city everything is glum
      and gritty,
  Life seems really such a pity that it isn't worth the
      while;
Ugliness and dirt assail you, smoke and evil odors
      trail you,
  All your cheery visions fail you, and you cannot
      crack a smile.
Streets seen full of people—dreary, tattered, battered,
      bleak and bleary,
  Everybody makes you weary, every prospect makes
      you blue,
No one says or smiles a "howdy!" every one is drab or
      dowdy,
  When the city's gray and cloudy—it just frowns and
      frowns at you!

When it's sunny in the city every girl you see is
      pretty,
  Every fellow's wise or witty, every Jack is with his
      Jill;
Everybody's happy, happy, from the hobo to the
      chappy,
  Every footstep's brisk and snappy, every heartbeat
      is a thrill!

SHADE AND LIGHT (continued)

Laughter lilts and young blood races, tragedy has left
    no traces,
    Everywhere are lovely faces most alluring to the
      view,
Poll, and Doll, and Prue, and Kitty—oh, this life's a
    tuneful ditty
    When it's sunny in the city, and the city smiles at
      you!

FALSE BEACONS

OH, the night lights, the white lights,
   That will not let me go,
That glare and flare upon the air
   And beckon to me so;
The mad lights, the glad lights,
   That bind me to the town,
They're cheering when I'm on the crest
   And sneering when I'm down!

The white lights, the bright lights
   That blaze against the sky!
The call of them, the thrall of them
   When life is running high!
The gay lights, the play lights
   Above the surge and press,
They're crowning wealth with radiance
   And frowning on distress!

The white lights, the night lights!
   How wondrously they shine
Upon the jewels and the silks,
   The women and the wine!
The bold lights, the cold lights,
   The city's magic lure,
They never gave me faith or love,
   Yet they enslave me sure!

THOSE BENEATH THE HARROW

THE WORKING SONG

(After Chesterton)

OH, we're sick to death of the style of song
  That's only a sort of a simpering song,
A kissy song and a sissy song
  Or a weepy, creepy, whimpering song.
So give us the lift of a lusty song,
  A boisterous, bubbling, boiling song,
Or a smashing song and a dashing song,
  Oh, give us the tang of a toiling song,
The chanty loud of the working crowd,
  The thunderous thrall of a toiling song!

Ay, sing us a joyous daring song,
  Not a moaning, groaning, fretting song,
But a ringing song, and a swinging song,
  A rigorous, vigorous, sweating song.
We have had enough of the gypsy song,
  Which is only a lazy, shirking song,
So toughen your throat to a rougher note
  And give us the tune of a working song,
A tune of strife and the joy of life,
  The beat and throb of a working song!

THE OLD TIMER

YEP, this here camp is the pink of propriety,
    Calm and respectable, lawful an' clean,
Ten story buildin's an' high class society
    Lends quite a cultured effect to the scene.
Doubtless these days of the present is bully days,
    We got a right to be proud of our style,
Yet—we do hanker fer raw wild-an'-woolly days,
        Onct in a while!

Onct in a while we old timers gets wonderin'
    Whether life hadn't more zip in the past,
When this here city was roarin' an' thunderin',
    Gamblin' an' drinkin' an' fightin' full blast.
Wicked, them times, with a lot that was black to them,
    Lawless an' rough, yet how fondly we smile,
When we are sort of rememberin' back to them,
        Onct in a while.

Then, while we doubtless was wild, unregenerate,
    Each man was free, though he might be a scamp;
Now, with the laws an' conventions we venerate,
    Companies owns us—an' bosses the camp.
Maybe it's true these is finer an' better days,
    Freer of trouble, though fuller of guile,
Still—a man dreams of them brave old red-letter days
        Onct in a while.

THE OLD TIMER (continued)

Gen'rally speakin', To-day has the best of it,
   All us old mossbacks is stubborn, that's all,
Wantin' the past when, if we was possessed of it,
   Prob'ly it wouldn't be like we recall;
Still—we looks back on its tumult an' strife again,
   Days when each miner was blowin' his pile,
Hungerin', thirstin', to taste the old life again—
    Onct in a while.

BACK IN THE STATES

WE have wholly forsaken the tropics,
  We are back to "God's country" again,
Where we talk about commonplace topics
  And we mingle with everyday men.
We are done with Gatun and Gorgona,
  Away from Culebra we've blown,
But in secret we frequently own a
  Decided desire for the Zone.

The Zone, with its glum and its glad men,
  Whose brains with one thought were athrob,
The Zone, with its glorious madmen
  Who ate, drank, and slept with "the job,"
Whose talk was of "slides" and of "levels,"
  Of "seepage" and "channels" and "fills,"
A crew of maniacal devils—
  Oh, Lord, how the memory thrills!

The wind's blowing cold and we shiver,
  And somehow we seem to recall
The days by the old Chagres River,
  The nights in the new Corazal,
The tropical moon in its beauty,
  And the trade blowing gentle and bland,
And the stars doing sentinel duty
  As they watched over Spiggoty Land.

BACK IN THE STATES (continued)

How they winked down on Panama City
    And blinked on its ways from above,
Its priests and its smiling banditti,
    Its lights and its laughter and love;
They saw how we spent and we sported,
    They know how we loafed and we lied,
They know who the girls were we courted—
    And most of the Zone did, beside.

We worked—and we put our whole heart in,
    And swift was the pace we were hurled,
For we knew we were all taking part in
    The mightiest job in the world;
Now back in the "States" you will find us,
    Where life is of different tone,
And the other is well left behind us—
    But, say, what's the news from the Zone?

MAN MUSIC

I HAVE heard a lot of music in my time,
  From the classic to the hurdy-gurdy tune,
From the operatic aria sublime
  To the sentimental ballad to the moon;
But the music that will stir me to the core,
  And that fills my nerves and arteries with thrills,
Is the syncopated thunder and the roar
  And the heavy ragtime rhythm of the drills!

In the low and dripping heading with its murk
  Where the oil lights smoke and flicker, fade and flare,
I can hear the air drills settling to their work,
  And it makes me half way crazy to be there,
With the piston shaking underneath my hand
  As it batters at the everlasting hills;
It's a music that I love and understand
  When I hear the ragtime rhythm of the drills!

Yes, the drills, they hammer, hammer and they thud,
  As they break the peace of ages underground
In a rhythm that goes throbbing through the blood
  In a deafening intensity of sound;
It's a siren song that holds me in a thrall,
  And it racks me like the fever and the chills,
And it drowns all other voices with its call,
  With the loud and ragtime rhythm of the drills!

MAN MUSIC (continued)

Oh, the drills, they put a tingle in my feet,
    And they set my body swaying to and fro
As they batter and they thunder and they beat
    On the battlements of nature, down below;
It's a wild and raucous music at the best,
    But there's something in my being it fulfills,
And my heart is keeping tempo in my chest
    To the syncopated rhythm of the drills.
Yes, a miner feels a longing in his breast
    When he hears the ragtime rhythm of the drills!

THE BREAD LINE

WELL, here they are—they stand and stamp and
shiver,
  Waiting their food from some kind stranger hand,
Their weary limbs with eagerness aquiver
  Hungry and heartsick in a bounteous land.

"Beggars and bums?" Perhaps, and largely worthless,
  Shaky with drink, unlovely, craven, low,
With obscene tongues and hollow laughter mirthless,
  But who shall give them scorn for being so?

Yes, here they are—with gaunt and pallid faces,
  With limbs ill-clad and fingers stiff and blued,
Shuffling and stamping on their pavement places,
  Waiting and watching for their bit of food.

We boast of vast achievement and of power,
  Of human progress knowing no defeat,
Of strange new marvels every day and hour—
  And here's the bread line in the wintry street!

Ten thousand years of war and peace and glory,
  Of hope and work and deeds and golden schemes,
Of mighty voices raised in song and story,
  Of huge inventions and of splendid dreams.

THE BREAD LINE (continued)

Ten thousand years replete with every wonder,
  Of empires risen and of empires dead,
Yet still, while wasters roll in swollen plunder,
  These broken men must stand in line—for bread!

THE EMPIRE BUILDER

HE built a railroad through the wilderness,
  And built it largely by his own sheer might
Of courage and of daring and of brain.
(Of course some ten or twenty thousand men
And women put their money into stock
Which gave him capital to build the road,
And other thousands sweat or schemed for him,
But none the less the credit rightly goes
To him for putting through his visioned plan.)

He built a railroad through the wilderness,
Then, having built it, made the rates so high
That mining, agriculture, business groaned
Beneath the load, and still survived
Only because the country was so rich.
Because he wanted cash—and cash at once,
And couldn't see much further than his nose,
He'd grab a thousand dollars in a rush
Although it cost him fifty thousand more
A few years later. And he'd pat himself
Upon the back for being very smart.
Where lower rates would have built up a town,
Developed industry and meant, in time,
Millions of dollars every year to him,
He'd keep the tariffs where they were, because
They brought a few more thousand dollars then,
Though they might ruin any future trade.

THE EMPIRE BUILDER (continued)

Sometimes his gouging tactics were so harsh
That people ceased to ship upon his line,
And sent their goods on creaking wagon trains
Through rocky mountain passes. Even then
It took him months and months to see the light.
You would have thought his railroad line, once built,
Was something perfect and immutable,
The way he fought improvement. Day by day
And year by year, the people fought and fought
(By law, by pressure and by boycott, too),
To push his tariffs down, his service up,
And thus by constant, unremitting war
They made his road a highway unto wealth
For all the country where his rails were laid.
(And incidentally they made for him
—This empire builder—much against his will,
Millions on millions.) Thus the empire grew
Although he blindly fought to check its growth,
Because he couldn't see beyond his nose.
Yet when he died the papers all declared,
"He built an empire. With a vision vast
Created cities, villages and farms,
Trade, manufacture, commerce, power and wealth.
He was a Seer, Builder, Master-Mind."
The truth is that the pulsing empire grew
By economic forces—forces which
He tried to fight and never understood,
And which made him a multi-millionaire
Against his frantic struggles. Thus we find
That his achievement—great enough, in truth,
And worthy of full praise—was simply this,
"He built a railroad through the wilderness!"

SAVOUR OF SALT

TO MY FUTURIST LOVE

(Fashion declares that women shall wear pink and blue hair and paint their faces in various startling hues.)

HOW shall I praise thee in verses ecstatical,
    Light of my Spirit and Queen of my Heart,
Lady of pulchritude polychromatical,
    Ultimate triumph of Futurist art?
Time was I caroled of locks that were aureate,
    Raved of your eyes that were limpid and blue,
Now though I sing with the skill of a laureate,
    How can I properly celebrate you?

You with the hair that is blue or carnelian,
    Purple or orange—according to styles—
Making a mock of the well-known chameleon,
    Beating the spectrum by several miles;
Lips that are yellow and cheeks that are violet,
    Eyebrows and lashes a beautiful pink—
How can I lilt them in ballad or triolet
    When I have only one color of ink?

Druggists have raided the realms pharmaceutical
    Seeking for pigments and powders and paint
Which would impart to your hair and your cuticle
    Colors to make a kaleidoscope faint.

TO **MY FUTURIST LOVE** (continued)
Yes, you are lovely—and yet I prefer **to go**
Far, far away from this Futurist guise;
Gazing upon you has given me vertigo—
Lady, you're *fearfully* hard on my eyes!

THE CONFESSION

IN public, of course, I must bear myself ever
As modest in all that I am or I do;
In private I think I'm decidedly clever,
Excelled, if at all, by a fortunate few.
In public I rave over other folk's labors,
And wish I could do things as finely as they;
But when I'm alone, I look down on my neighbors
And think of myself as superior clay.

In public I giggle at other men's chatter;
To brilliance in banter I take off my hat;
In private I sneer: "What a cheap line of patter!
My dullest remarks are much brighter than that."
In public I say, "I'm a mere poetaster
Who writes little rhymes for the people to see";
But really I think I'm a regular master,
That Shakspere and Byron have nothing on me.

For public consumption it's clearly my duty
To speak of my looks with a modesty vast;
In private I think that my fine, manly beauty
Has Mr. Adonis lashed tight to the mast.
In public I place, with immense circumspection,
My thoughts egotistical back on the shelf;
In private I think myself near to perfection.
Well, don't *You* feel that way concerning your-
self?

[95]

PREPAREDNESS

WE are made of dust, so the preachers say,
  And we only live for a little day,

And then, regardless of wealth or fame,
Return to the dirt from whence we came.

However we live, at last we go
Into the dust that the breezes blow.

Ah well, drink up! let us never fret,
If we keep our gullets extremely wet

Our dust may prove so damp to touch
That the wind can't blow us about so much!

LOGIC

I LOVED a girl in days of yore,
  A girl who said me nay
Because she loved Another more—
  That's why I went away!

And then I wandered everywhere
  About this earthly ball
And met a lot of maidens fair,
  Who held my heart in thrall.

For there were girls in Kankakee
  And girls in Rio, too.
Wherever chance has landed me
  Were pretty girls to woo,

In Boston Town or far Japan,
  In Panama and Nome,
But each one loved another man—
  And that's why I came home!

THE WHISTLER

"One of the worst pests is the dinged fool who whistles in public places, street cars, busses, etc., to the annoyance of every one around him. A licking is none too good for him."—A Letter to the Editor.

WHISTLE, old chap; you just go on and whistle;
   Never you fret about kickers like him;
Your heart's as light as the down of a thistle;
   Who cares if grumblers are grouchy and grim?
Go on and whistle; don't mind what they say to you;
   Most of us thrill to your message of cheer;
Fortune is good and the world's looking gay to you?
   Go on and whistle; it's pleasant to hear!
Whistle, man, whistle—as light as a thistle;
   Go on and whistle; it's bully to hear!

Whistle, old fellow; you go on and whistle;
   What do we care if you sharp or you flat?
Let the old bachelors burble and bristle;
   Who gives a whoop for such people as that?
Go on and whistle—it proves there is Boy in you.
   Youth that has lasted for many a year,
Give us the notes of the fun and the joy in you;
   Go on and whistle; it's pleasant to hear;
Whistle, man, whistle, as light as a thistle;
   Go on and whistle—it's bully to hear!

THE WHISTLER (continued)

Whistle, old chap—you just go on and whistle;
   Give us your flutings of popular airs;
Whistle in spite of the grouches who bristle;
   Whistle away all our worries and cares;
Something there is of the troubadour clan in you
   Warming our hearts with your melodies clear;
Toil is forgot as we hark to the Pan in you;
   Go on and whistle—it's pleasant to hear;
Whistle, man, whistle—as light as a thistle;
   Go on and whistle—it's bully to hear!

AMBITION

(The Humorist)

IF I could spring one cosmic joke,
    To make the whole world's midriff quake
        With one stupendous burst of glee,
Till every kind and race of folk—
        The Russ, the Celt, the dull Chinee—
    Would hold their trembling sides and shake—
If I could girdle all the earth
With one Gargantuan blast of mirth,
And set each windowpane and rafter
Aquiver with the echoed laughter—
If I could pen one cosmic jape,
    To make the sick man on his couch,
The widow in her new-bought crape
        (Bedewed with many a salty tear),
    The old dyspeptic with his grouch,
        The cynic with his constant sneer—
To make these give, first, just a grin;
Then, as the jest sunk deeper in,
A gurgle of a joyous sort;
And then a titter; then a snort;
And then, as from their very core,
A bellowing and gorgeous roar;
If I could make the whole world howl,
With panting sides and aching jowl—
That would fill up my cup of bliss,
Nor would I ask for more than this.

AMBITION (continued)

> Kingdoms and empires manifold
> Or riches vast to bulge my purse
> Would tempt me not, if I might hold
> The title of the Master Clown
> And Jester to the Universe!

THE ATAVISTIC MAID

LISTEN, Sweetheart, to my plea;
  Cut this highly cultured game.
All this fine gentility
  Grows to be exceeding tame.
What *I* want is low-brow love,
  Heavy, knockdown cave-man stuff;
I'm no cooing turtle dove;
  Treat me rough, kid; treat me rough!

Can the soft and weepy sighs,
  Chop the meek and humble pose.
I'm no cut-glass raffle prize,
  I'm no fragile little rose!
Grab me with a python grip.
  If I struggle, call the bluff.
Want my love? Then take the tip,
  Treat me rough, kid; treat me rough!

I don't want my hand caressed
  With a nice respectful peck;
Yank me wildly to your chest;
  If I fight you, break my neck.
Please don't be a gentle dub,
  Spilling la-de-dah-ish guff,
Woo and win me with a club.
  Treat me rough, kid; treat me rough!

LUXURY

CONCEPTIONS of affluence vary a lot;
  To one man it's victuals and drink;
Another man dreams of a sea-going yacht,
  With a music room finished in pink;
To women it often means gems by the peck,
  But affluence spells—to my brain—
A car where you sit on the back of your neck
  And drive with an air of disdain.

You've seen just the type of an auto I mean;
  It's long and it's throbbing with might;
It's built very much like a sleek submarine,
  But it runs like an aero in flight;
In brief it's the kind that can certainly "trek"
  When it roars like a limited train,
The car where you sit on the back of your neck
  And drive with an air of disdain.

I might be so broke that I'd skimp on my meals
  And pawn all my shirt studs for "gas,"
But if I could own such a monarch on wheels
  I'd think of myself as "the class."
Of debts and of poverty little I'd reck,
  For an affluent poise I'd maintain
In a car where you sit on the back of your neck
  And drive with an air of disdain!

[103]

BALLADS OF WHAT YOU PLEASE

BASEBALL

IF you've never sat in the blazing sun and prayed the
gods for another run,
    If you're not clean daft till the season's done and
        the talk of the game is through,
If you've never joined in the bleachers' roar at a double
      play or a daring score,
    Don't listen to this a minute more, this ballad is not
        for you!

But if the sound of the ball that's hit or the thump of
      a strike in the catcher's mitt,
    And the umpire's voice and the coacher's wit are
        spells that hold you sure,
If you're one of the faithful, cheering throng that fol-
      lows the fate of the team along
    Maybe you'll join in the swinging song, the song of
        the baseball lure!

        Chuck-full of glamour,
        Tumult and clamor,
Sparkling with vigor and zipping with zest.
        Gingery, tangy,
        Flippant, and slangy,
Brimful of action and banter and jest.
Sport of the multitude—held by its joys again,
Staidest of people are nothing but boys again!

BASEBALL (continued)

In every city or country spot, in every corner or vacant lot,
    In any old weather, cool or hot, from earliest spring to fall,
The young and lively, the old and gray, are there to join or watch the play,
    The game that wields its royal sway and keeps the land in thrall.

And if you're watching the players sweat, down on the field where the scene is set,
    You feel its magic and you forget your age and your sense as well.
For the game—it turns your face to tan, it makes a boy of the oldest man,
    It turns the sane to a crazy fan with nothing to do but yell!

        Calling for muscle,
        Hurry, and hustle,
Baseball's a tussle that's vivid with vim,
        Heated but happy,
        Peaceful but scrappy,
Evermore snappy and nevermore grim!
Sport of the multitude—every one's wild again,
Every true fan is as young as a child again.

Oh, the silence tense and the hush of doubt with the bases full and two men out,
    And the clean, sharp hit, and the rooters' shout as the runners cross the plate,

BASEBALL (continued)

Or the long-drawn "Ah!" as the ball soars high and
the fielder shields his sun-dazed eye
And waits and gathers the falling fly as certain and
sure as fate,

Oh, the jeers, the cheers, and the throbbing thrill, the
batter's might and the pitcher's skill,
The crowd that never is wholly still but shouting its
joy or woe,
These are the things that fan the flame, that lend their
wonder to the game,
That make it glorious in its fame, the king of all
games we know!

Free of the grafter,
Lighted with laughter,
Full of the spirit of never say die!
Action is in it
Every sharp minute,
Something is doing to capture the eye!
Then—and the reason can never be hid again—
Best of it is—that it makes you a kid again!

PAN

PAN'S piping still, as blithe and bold
  As in the dreamful days of old;
 Adown the vale, atop the hill,
 You hear his melodies that thrill
With lyric raptures manifold,
        Pan's piping still!

His joyous visage you behold,
Crinkling with merriment untold,
   And from his lips the bird-notes spill,
        Pan's piping still.

A creature of the wild and wold
Made in the ancient pagan mold—
   A Boy, with puckered lips that trill
   Their magic message clear and shrill,
Youth brings us back the Age of Gold,
        Pan's piping still!

THE FLAG

IS it, then, only a tricolored rag,
  As the street-corner orators say of it?
Maybe it isn't worth loving—the flag,
  For all of the pomp and display of it;
But though I grow cynical, callous, and wise,
  I cannot think lightly or ill of it;
Whenever, wherever it comes to my eyes
  I feel all the glamour and thrill of it.

The toil of the hands that have wrought for it,
The blood of the soldiers that fought for it,
  Are part of its wonderful story,
This banner unfurled to the winds of the world,
    Old Glory!

Maybe it isn't worth loving at all,
  The red and the blue and the white of it;
Maybe "Tradition" has got me in thrall
  When I grow proud at the sight of it;
Still, when that banner is flung to the breeze,
  How the heart warms to the gleam of it!
Still, when you're sailing on far-away seas,
  How you can long for and dream of it!

How can you censure our pride for it?
Thousands have struggled and died for it,
  Weaving its marvelous story,
This banner unfurled to the winds of the world,
    Old Glory!

AN IDEAL

I WISH I were as trig a man,
  As big a man,
    As bright a man;
I wish I were as *right* a man in all this earthly show,
    As broad and high and long a man,
      As strong a man,
        As fine a man,
As pretty near divine a man as one I used to know.

    I wish I were as grave a man,
      As brave a man,
        As keen a man,
As learned and serene a man, as fair to friend and foe.
    I wish I owned sagaciousness
      And graciousness
        As should a man
Who hopes to be as good a man as one I used to know.

    I'd be a creature glorious,
      Victorious,
        A Wonder-man,
Not just a sort of Blunder-man whose ways and
  thoughts are slow.
    If I could only be the man,
      One-tenth of one degree the man,
I used to think my father was when I was ten or so.

JACK LONDON

An Appreciation

HERE'S to you, Jack, whose virile pen
  Concerns itself with Man's Size Men;
Here's to you, Jack, whose stories thrill
  With savor of the western breeze,
With magic of the south—and chill
  Shrill winds from icy floes and seas;
You have not wallowed in the mire
And muck of tales of foul desire,
For, though you've sung of fight and fraud,
  Of love and hate—ashore, afloat—
  You have not struck a ribald note
Nor made your art a common bawd.

Here's to you, Jack; I've loved your best,
  Your finest stories from the first,
Your sagas of the north and west—
  But what is more—I've loved your worst!
For, in the poorest work you do,
There's something clean and strong and true,
A tang of big and primal things,
  A sweep of forces vast and free,
A touch of wizardry which brings
  The glamour of the wild to me.

JACK LONDON (continued)
>So when I read a London tale
>Forthwith I'm set upon a trail
>Of great enchantment, and I track
>Adventure round the world and back,
>With you for guide—here's to you, Jack.

TO BOOTH TARKINGTON, MASTER PENMAN

TARKINGTON, how shall we carol the worth of
   you,
  Master of marvelous magical prose?
How shall we sing of the humor and mirth of you?
  How shall we warble the art you disclose?
You who have stirred us to love or frivolity,
  Wound us up tight in your magical snare,
You who have written of plain folks and "quality,"
  Cherry and Penrod and Monsieur Beaucaire?

"Will o' the Wisp, with a flicker of Puck in you,"
  Thus warbled Hovey of Barney McGee.
Sure you have all of his charm and good luck in you,
  Mixed with a genius dazzling to see,
Love and philosophy, wisdom and joy in you;
  All these we know, but we love most of all
Just the unquenchable spirit of Boy in you,
  Blithe with the days that we'd like to recall.

You haven't dug in the muck of society
  Seeking for filth to be shown us as "Life,"
Yet you have pictured in flashing variety
  Tragedy, comedy, glamour and strife;
Here's to you, Tarkington, Humanitarian,
  Humanist, rather, with eyes that are clear;
May you live long as a hale centenarian,
  Writing more bully good tales every year!

GUESS WHO?

SOMETIMES fantastical,
  Often bombastical,
Always dynamic and never scholastical,
    Slightly uproarious,
    Bracing as Boreas,
Living each day with a zest that is glorious,
Bane of the highbrows and folk hypercritical,
    Subject of many a plutocrat's curse,
Buried in state by his foemen political
    Only to climb up and pilot the hearse!

There is an air to him,
There's such a flare to him,
There's such a rare, debonair do-and-dare to him!
    Bull dog tenacity,
    Mixed with vivacity,
Tempered with humor and sense and sagacity;
What if his speeches are crowded with platitudes,
    Somehow he's built on the popular plan,
Actions and manner and sayings and attitudes,
    All of them prove him a Regular Man!

Quite undistressable,
Most irrepressible,
Open and frank—yet a problem unguessable,
    Terse, though didactical,
    Learned, but practical,
Strong for preparedness, moral and tactical,

GUESS WHO? (continued)

    Vivid and vital and vervy and vigorous,
        Simply and humanly "playing the game,"
    Preaching and living a life that is rigorous,
    ——Give you three guesses to call him by name!

CPSIA information can be obtained
at www.ICGtesting.com
Printed in the USA
LVOW04s0016140816
500277LV00019B/917/P